In This Life

Life

Spiritual Growth
and Aging

In This Life

Spiritual Growth and Aging

Leo Missinne, PhD

Liguori
LIGUORI, MISSOURI

Imprimi Potest:
Harry Grile, CSsR, Provincial
Denver Province, The Redemptorists

Published by Liguori Publications
Liguori, Missouri 63057

To order, call 800-325-9521
www.liguori.org

Library of Congress Cataloging-in-Publication Data

Missinne, Leo.
 In this life : spiritual growth and aging / Leo Missinne. — First
Edition.
  pages cm
1. Older Christians—Religious life. 2. Older people—Religious
life. 3. Middle-aged persons—Religious life. 4. Aging—Religious
aspects—Christianity. 5. Aging. I. Title.
 BV4580.M55 2013
 248.8'5—dc23

                                                              2013016070

pISBN: 978-0-7648-2367-1
eISBN: 978-0-7648-6869-6

Liguori Publications, a nonprofit corporation, is an apostolate of
The Redemptorists. To learn more about The Redemptorists, visit
Redemptorists.com.

Printed in the United States of America
17 16 15 14 13 / 5 4 3 2 1
First Edition

Contents

Preface

This book offers no ready-made recipes or advice about staying in good health and in good physical shape in spite of age like the commercials promise. On the contrary, these pages invite readers to take old age fully; to discover the value of the third phase of life; to give, in short, a more profound meaning to earthly existence until its very last moments.

Growing in age is a path of progress (in the strong sense of the word) that allows many positive aspects often neglected in present society despite inevitable physical and psychological problems. The attitude that one can have vis-à-vis the process of growing old will depend, then, directly on the manner of envisioning life, suffering, and death, and on the meaning one gives them. Seen in this light, old age is not a problem but a possibility.

This book is only a beginning; the reader has to complete and finish it. My sources of information are my conversations with God, friends, colleagues, and older people. I am most grateful to all of my gerontology students at the University of Nebraska and the University of Southern California. They have been a source of inspiration. My contacts with so many wise older people opened a door for looking toward older age as a time of wisdom and grace.

The ideas, lectures and readings of Viktor E. Frankl's books have inspired my ideas in this book.

Viktor E. Frankl, *Man's Search for Meaning.* Boston: Beacon Press, 1985.

Viktor E. Frankl, *The Doctor of the Soul,* NewYork: Bantam Books, 1985.

Viktor E. Frankl, *Psychotherapy and Existentialisme*, NewYork: Touch-stone, 1985.

In Search of the Meaning of Life

Does life still have meaning for someone who reaches advanced age? That question is not easy to answer. A double reflection is required, as much about life itself as about old age. Life is one of the most mysterious realities. When we add the complicated givens of extreme old age to the search for the meaning of life, we are confronted with a problem of rare complexity.

No science will ever be able to unveil the deep meaning of old age. Aging is only an incomplete aspect of the reality we call life. Life belongs to the order of mystery, not to the field of problems. We can analyze and explain problems by a system of considerations about motives and purposes, means and consequences.

But only a thoughtful attitude permits access to mysteries, and they never give up the totality of their secrets. Mysteries are part of God's gifts to humankind. That is why respect is the only appropriate attitude in confronting a mystery; in wishing to elucidate the mystery scientifically, we end up killing it.

Explain or contemplate?

Let's suppose that a being from another world lands on Earth. Scientists could analyze it, dissect it, and thereby gather innumerable data, which would be greatly appreciated in the scientific world. But would they have explained this extraterrestrial? No, for to be able to examine and analyze it in that manner, it would have to be put to death. Of course, we would have understood its composition and its functioning, but we would have killed it!

Too much science and too many techniques are mortally dangerous for what is really important: living and communicating with others. That is why I prefer to approach our subject from the angle of an interior reflection, without attempting to dismantle the works of an entire mechanism. The most fundamental question concerning old age—the question of meaning—is not in the purview of science. It is a philosophical question that has, moreover, numerous implications in the very real lives of today's men and women.

Old age is a period of life in which we can cast a retrospective look on an entire life. Things take their place in a wider frame. This look back, it is true, will never be able to include the whole of existence. But at the moment we glimpse the end of the road and when our task is nearly achieved, we feel a real need to understand the meaning of all we have lived. Then questions loom: *Why have I lived? Why do I still live, fragile, sick, or handicapped as I am? What good is it to live like this? Why should I continue to live in a society that, as a matter of fact, has already excluded me?*

These thoughts are familiar to a great many elderly persons, as well as to those who care for them. These questions must not be rejected. By suggesting several answers, we will probably be able to help people live their situation in a more dignified and humane manner.

One question, several answers

The answers to the question of the meaning of life are extremely varied and often contradictory. The wise Buddha taught that we must immerse ourselves in the river of life and leave the question of meaning to resolve itself. Existentialist Jean-Paul Sartre asserts that human life arises by neither design nor significance, that it continues out of weakness, and is snuffed out by chance. (According to Sartre, birth and death are equally deprived of significance.)

The Russian writer Leo Tolstoy confesses to having been tormented all his life by this quest for meaning: "The question, which in my fiftieth year had brought me to the notion of suicide, was the simplest of all questions, lying in the soul of every man from the undeveloped child to wisest sage: 'What will come from what I am doing now, and may do tomorrow? What will come from my whole life?' otherwise expressed, 'Why should I live? Why should I wish for anything? Why should I do anything?' Again, in other words: 'Is there any meaning in my life which will not be destroyed by the inevitable death awaiting me?'"

And further on he writes again: "Five years ago a strange state of mind began to grow upon me: I had moments of perplexity, of a stoppage, as it were, of life, as if I did not know how I was to live, what I was to do....These stoppages of life always presented themselves to me with the same question: Why? and what for?...These questions demanded an answer with greater and greater persistence and like dots, grouped themselves into one black spot."

French author and philosopher Albert Camus believed all people are looking for a "why" they never find and are doomed to live in absurdity. He was convinced that many people die because life for them was not worth living. From this he concluded that the question of life's meaning is the most urgent of all, even if it is never to be resolved.

Finding life's meaning is good for your health

Many psychologists agree that a lack of meaning in life, or meaninglessness, is often the origin of neurotic or psychotic behavior. Carl Jung felt that the clinical syndrome of meaninglessness was a very common phenomenon in his practice as a psychiatrist. He wrote: "Absence of meaning in life plays a crucial role in the etiology of neurosis." Every neurosis must be understood, ultimately, as the suffering of a soul that has not discovered its meaning. Thus he said that most of his patients were not suffering from any clinically definable neurosis, but only from the "senselessness and aimlessness of their lives."

Psychiatrist Viktor E. Frankl stated that most of his patients suffered from an existential neurosis, which had meaninglessness at its root. Many contemporary psychologists are of the same opinion: the lack of purpose in life is what is found most often at the base of deviant or abnormal conduct.

But we do not need to be famous psychologists to see the deadly role of meaninglessness. Meaninglessness is manifested in the disease of our time—boredom. People today find everything boring: their studies, their profession, their marriage, their friends, even their vacations! For this reason, many (the youngest ages especially) seek compensation in fast-paced activities, alcohol, or drugs to feel they are living. Such behavior helps them feel they have a purpose in life for at least a few hours or days, until the artificial excitement disappears and they find themselves back in the pit. Others dress in extravagant clothes or dye their hair or buy fancy possessions to have that sense of meaning.

We cannot escape it. Everyone, at least at certain times, seeks a valid and fulfilling meaning for life. It is the painful privilege of being human, for we are the only living beings who can reflect. Such questions are peculiar to us, whether young or old. These questionings can sometimes assume tragic proportions, such as when one is ill, when one suffers the loss of a relative or friend, or when one feels the end of life is near.

And then there is Sigmund Freud. He didn't consider this quest for meaning a motivation, a privilege typical of human beings. Rather, he saw the quest as a deviation peculiar to old age, an unhealthy manifestation and the proof of an interior disorder. According to him, the very fact of asking ourselves questions about the meaning of life prevented finding it and constituted a symptom of failure. In this view, elderly persons became pathological cases.

In that matter, Freud is fundamentally wrong. The quest for meaning is an essential part of being human: we want to make something of our life and of our world, we want to achieve something significant. If we don't succeed at that, we risk falling into distressing if not tragic situations—from depression to suicide.

Guideposts on the road of meaning

No psychologist can give us better information, better directives for making progress on the road of meaning, than Viktor Frankl. His theory furnishes a solid foundation to explain the different crises of life, and especially the crises of elderly persons at the time of their retirement, upon the death of their life companion, or more simply, when they take stock of the multiple restrictions and sufferings inherent in old age.

Each crisis provides an opportunity to look for new answers to questions like, *Why did this ordeal have to fall on me? Haven't I always done my best? Why must I have to go on suffering so much now that I have grown old?* The surprising thing is that most often it is not success or the experiencing of happiness that incites us to ask ourselves the fundamental questions; rather, failure and suffering incite the questions.

At that moment the old certitudes are called into question and a purification can come about. This is what Frankl clearly demonstrates in his successful book *Man's Search for Meaning.* The author describes his experiences in his role as doctor-prisoner in a Nazi concentration camp and tries to rationally understand the experiences.

As a professor of psychiatry and neurology at the University of Vienna, Frankl did not take issue with the eminent psychoanalysts who preceded him, namely, Freud, Adler, and Jung. He subscribed to the importance Freud attached to sexuality. He was in agreement with the specific aspects of Adler's theory: the will to power and the need to assert oneself. He also agreed with the majority of Jung's views.

But above all, Frankl was convinced that the need to give meaning to life is the most fundamental of all human needs and the one that liberates the greatest number of forces for action. According to him, life can always find a motivation, even in the worst circumstances, like in a concentration camp. He had discovered that human beings were able to bear unspeakable suffering if they just had a goal, an incentive to survive. It was often the will to see one's wife, husband, or children again, or eventually to write a book on the conditions of life of the departed. By putting the need to give meaning to existence above all other needs, Frankl changed the face of psychoanalysis and made of this need a profoundly human theory.

The importance of values

Frankl was of the opinion that men and women succeed in giving meaning to their life in terms of the values they attribute to it. These are the values that make their life significant and often explain their behavior. Frankl distinguishes three important categories of values: creative, experiential, and attitudinal.

When someone wants to carry out something in his or her life, like writing a book, building a house, recruiting a group of volunteers, organizing a celebration, painting, playing music, or studying, that person carries out values of creativity. In other words, a person has to do something—create something—to find meaning in life. Undertaking a project for some thing or someone—one's family, the community, or the Church—and having a precise goal are evident means of giving meaning to life. Living an active life serves the purpose of giving opportunities to realize values through creative work—through making a new creation. It is especially important for the elderly to be able to attain these values of creativity by conceiving and realizing projects. It helps to spend this phase of life in a meaningful way.

Next to the values of creativity, Frankl places the values of experience. Experiential values are lived by knowing a single human being in all his or her uniqueness. But in a more general way, the pursuit of goodness, truth, and beauty also provides fertile ground for the flowering of these values, as well as a feeling of fulfillment. If someone has become unique, incomparable, and irreplaceable in your eyes, the experience of such a love gives ample reason to want to continue living. Reciprocal love between a man and a woman gives deep meaning to the lives of many and gives them the courage to continue to live, in spite of everything. We want to live as long as possible for and with the one we love. Love of grandchildren gives many older people a deep sense of satisfaction that can add meaning and even years to their lives. And it is the love of God and zeal for the Church that continue to inspire so many priests and religious, even at an advanced age, and give meaning to their lives.

Experiential values are realized not only through love and goodness but also in the constant pursuit—even at an advanced age—of truth. People want to live according to what they believe to be valid and true. This is important not only for the elderly but also for the young people who find a model in them. In a world full of lies and deceit, the elderly concerned about rectitude and truth provide an example and permanent invitation for the young to adopt the same values.

The experience of beauty in nature, art, or the aesthetic can be a source of profound satisfaction for older persons. Life is no longer stripped of meaning, and time spent appreciating one's surroundings begins to take on significance.

And so we come to the values of attitude or behavior. Frankl illustrates this attitudinal-value theory with a story that is filled with wisdom for older people. A doctor friend had come to consult him because he could not come to terms with the loss of his wife. In the course of the conversation, Frankl asked him if he would have preferred that his wife survive him and that she endure the suffering and mourning. His friend answered at once, "I would never want her to suffer what I suffer now. It was better that she die first." From that moment, the mourning of that man took on a meaning, and his suffering became a love offering that permitted him to resume life with courage and confidence.

Everything depends on the attitude, the behavior, that we adopt in the face of what happens to us. By finding the right attitude in the event of illness, failure, and suffering we can continue to live in a meaningful way and become better. Suffering borne in a worthy manner constitutes one of the most beautiful human attitudes and calls for the highest values.

All of Frankl's theory on the subject of attitudes is not limited to the world of the elderly, though for these purposes, it is very pertinent to the aging. As a matter of fact, suffering and detachment are important to the attainment of the values of attitude, which take more and more space with the progression of age.

Giving meaningful answers

Frankl was convinced that we don't find the meaning of life from our own expectations but, rather, in our way of responding, of reacting to the events of existence. To live significantly is to give meaning to everything life brings us. A meaningful response is not made of sterile ruminations or chats, but in the pursuit of and realization of something valid or the right attitude that one adopts in the face of circumstances.

Even the elderly remain responsible for the answers they give the questions posed by life. Those who in the past have always behaved in a relatively good manner must now, having grown old, make an effort to hold the same line and to do even better. If the past was mediocre, we are called in our role as seniors to change course. We must make an effort to bring the right answers—the right conduct—to the questions of life. Old age is a challenge. It incites us to act like free beings and to answer in personal and truly human ways to all the problems inherent in this period of existence. Elderly people have the capacity (and the duty) to take up this challenge in a manner that will serve as a model and inspiration to their contemporaries and to young people.

Human existence can always, regardless of the circumstances, remain a bearer of meaning, even in the greatest misery, in mourning, and when face-to-face with death. But before the definitive meaning of a human life appears, one can experiment with provisional and fleeting meanings. So it is, for example, that in devoting oneself to compassion for the suffering of someone or, say, in listening to beautiful music that one can experience moments of great fulfillment. Old age is the time to unify these provisional values into an ultimate meaning. With the approach of death, each day, each hour, becomes the bearer of the infinite. Young people are generally absorbed by the immediate, and the search for final meaning hardly preoccupies them. Later, when work does not demand all their strength and they have free time, they will have more opportunities to reflect on the deeper meaning of events past and present.

C.S. Lewis, a renowned Cambridge professor, was of the opinion that human beings can perceive a glimmer of ultimate meaning more than once in the course of their existence. Thus he suggests that a sudden awareness of beauty, the momentary sense of a deep inner peace, or an experience of undefined longing all point toward a larger and more definitive meaning of life, a life in the direction toward God. Old age is just the privileged time when we can make all these pointers converge, like so many directional arrows, toward the great Mystery to come. It is just the moment too—conscious that we are approaching death—to establish our own balance sheet. Has our life made this world a little better?

Where to find these values?

A person does not always immediately experience the value in moments of true meaning. We must "dis(un)cover" them. A real dialogue can contribute greatly to discovering a deeper meaning. The meaning of things often unveils itself in conversation with another person. Older people need conversations where they can express what is important to them and to recount what they have done in the course of their lives. Many seniors are not even conscious of the beautiful things they have accomplished over the years; if one lends an attentive ear, how many important values would emerge? To be able to confide in a loving listener is a privileged way to discover one's own values and to discover everything that gives meaning to life.

Next to these conversations is a meditative and peaceful reflection on our inner lives and on the world that surrounds us. Values appear then, not instantaneously, but progressively. It can even happen that we need our whole life to discover what values have finally given meaning to our existence. Agitation, noise, and pressure, so characteristic of our society, are not propitious to such a discovery. Contemplation requires time, silence, and relaxation. These conditions are indispensable to this more meditative and contemplative approach to life. That is why it is so important that we all find a place to establish our personal little "desert." We need a time and a place in which to withdraw in the calm and remain alone with our thoughts.

This is not to say this is simple, for solitude frightens many people. Excuses readily present themselves, but it is important not to forget that just like there are portable radios, there are also these "movable little corners of desert" to which each of us can withdraw "in spirit," even in the middle of the greatest agitation.

Choice and the look back

Searching for the meaning of life is a real challenge. It implies numerous choices of conscience. The formation of our conscience, then, constitutes a particularly important aspect of our lives here as a whole. Children, the young, and adults must continually make choices based on the values that have been inculcated by our education. We have learned that to choose is always a risk. But it is a possibility that is reserved for human beings, even if the consequences can sometimes turn out wrong. Isn't it better to live in a world that can produce both a Hitler and a Mother Teresa than in a world in which each person would act like a robot programmed to execute commands imposed from the outside?

After having made decisions upon decisions throughout life—all seemingly in the direction toward a full life—it is good to verify that this direction is the right one. This is what is meant by "life review." For elderly persons in particular, it is very important to be able to cast a retrospective look on life, to be able to harmonize significant new aspects of the present with the values of the past. All the fleeting moments, glimpses of meanings, that have been given to decisions and experiences during the different periods of life must now be synthesized into a signifying ensemble that sums up the ultimate meaning of existence.

Such is the task—and also the privilege—of the aging. One can bring together all these different elements of lived experiences and make of them a coherent unity that will give meaning to the past and, consequently, the future. This task is never finished. Until our last breath or, better yet, until our last lucid moment, we will have to continue to choose, to decide, to take a stand, to be able to take on with courage and dignity all that this last phase of life reserves for us, including death.

No one can achieve that completely alone. Help and encouragement can come from anyone, in any given situation. The presence of someone capable of sustaining relationship with another greatly facilitates this discovery of ultimate meaning. Thus to recall the past, interiorize it, relive it in depth, constitutes one of the most important tasks of the final phase of existence.

Older individuals love to recall the past and speak willingly of all those experiences that have marked them. They claim their memory is growing weak and they are afraid of losing their past. They want to recapture at all costs the time that is fleeting, for it is this past that has fashioned their identity and now enriches them by new facets. We do not just *have* a past, we *are* our past. It is from this long-lived past life that the aged must envisage this brief future that remains for them, to give a meaning to all that will yet happen to them, including death, and thus to harmonize the totality of their existence.

Living and Suffering

No one speaks voluntarily of suffering, much less of the suffering of the aged. We prefer to delete it from the realm of our consciousness. And if it happens to strike us, we have a tendency to rebel, to lose courage, and we don't know much about how to integrate it into our lives. However, suffering is entirely a part of the life of elderly persons, which is in stark contrast to the idealized image of the older generation presented by the media. There, one sees only happy elders, resplendent with health, always on vacation and traveling from one exotic country to another.

The value of suffering has been depreciated in our modern Western culture. We cling to a utopian ideal of living without pain, suffering, or death. Our generation could be called the "valium generation," because we tend to look for the sedation of all pain—of all present and future sufferings. Yet suffering is a real part of life, and it becomes more evident in older age when one has to cope with many physical and psychosocial losses. Older people also feel suffering more deeply because they are often isolated from their communities, friends, and relatives and lack the physical strength to cope with that isolation.

We all suffer because we are all human beings; and knowing suffering means we know what it means to be happy. Happiness and suffering are like love and hate. They are not opposites; they are components of the same reality. Happiness always presumes the possibility of being able to suffer, and suffering can be the beginning of happiness. This is why some people are afraid to love someone and be happy—because there is always suffering in the experience of being loved and of loving another person. Experiencing happiness in the present can create the fear that one day in the future we will lose that happiness and suffer from all kinds of physical or spiritual pain.

When we dream of a world without suffering, we tend to forget that suffering is a part of the history of humanity. The capacity to suffer is the origin of realizing and transcending our own human nature. If we were not able to suffer, we would be lifeless stones. We would not be able to create, invent, or be happy because surviving difficult circumstances and finding solutions to problems are the beginning of all human development.

Author David Wendell Moller expressed this truth in "On the Value of Suffering in the Shadow of Death," explaining that if humanity is deprived of the capability to suffer, then it narrows the human experience. Engaging in life's experiences is what makes us fully alive, and that means dealing with everything, including suffering. He also says that feelings cannot be readily compartmentalized or turned on and off. By doing that with suffering, we lose the ability to feel and that denying any sort of suffering eliminates any chance for a human experience to have meaning. Ultimately, Moller is saying that without suffering, life becomes a "pseudo-experience"—banal and unfulfilling.

While we must allow suffering in our lives, we should also allow others to suffer as well. We all carry our crosses. Sometimes we are so busy carrying our own cross that we forget to look around us to see that others have theirs too. So many times we simply do not see that they are carrying heavy loads as well. The "brilliant" aspects of their existence blind us, and that prevents us from seeing the dull and painful side. No one traverses life without sufferings or problems. No age group is spared. One can suffer with variable intensity and at different moments throughout life, but children, adolescents, adults, and the aged must all face some form of suffering.

Suffering can also come about without cause or without any action on our part. It sometimes happens so external to our lives, and yet can still be the gravest and heaviest to bear. There is no reason for the cause of suffering. Suffering strikes good and generous people, without warning, without explanation. Why must the good sometimes suffer so much while everything seems to succeed for the wicked? There is a question without an answer that we will not be able to free ourselves from throughout our lives.

A unique task rooted in love

While our actions may not cause our own suffering, there are moments in which our experience is such that we endure the suffering of others (as noted above, we must bear one another's crosses). Viktor Frankl's book *Man's Search for Meaning* has touched the hearts of millions who have sought meaning in their sufferings. As a concentration camp survivor from World War II, Frankl knew what it meant to suffer and to endure the horrible suffering of his fellow prisoners. In his book, he shows us that it is possible to grow, even—in his case—in a concentration camp. Frankl reminds us that when we find it is our destiny to suffer, we must see our suffering as a task—a unique task—that no one else can do for us.

We must accept the fact that even in our suffering, we are unique and irreplaceable.

No one can or ever will be able to understand your suffering completely, and no one can relieve you from all your suffering. Each man and each woman among us must bear his or her own suffering. And that is because we remain fundamentally alone in suffering, which gives us the opportunity of being unique in the way in which we face our own personal distresses.

This is not to say we cannot suffer with others. Suffering is often a heavy burden. People sometimes say, "Now, it is really too much…." The only thing we can do for those who undergo such an ordeal is to suffer with them, to remain close by, to travel part of the road with them. It is a help to them, but it is also a support to us as well, for the sick can encourage, console, and inspire those surrounding the sick bed. Those who suffer do not stay above their own painful situation, but they are instead immersed in their suffering. The ill do not preach lessons to us, they don't moralize, but they offer something more important: they show us how they manage their own suffering in a positive manner.

To survive the most painful situations proves humanness in ourselves and our connection with others—not just because we want to survive or somehow "prove" ourselves, but because we love someone and someone loves us. For example, a mother and son living in the same house may feel alienated and isolated from each other while a husband and wife separated by an ocean feel extremely close. That is because they love each other. The suffering of being far away from the other may even create a deeper love relationship. To further demonstrate this, we can look at the experiences of two well-known authors, Antoine de Saint-Exupery and Martin Gray.

French author and aviator Antoine de Saint-Exupery once lost his way while flying through a blizzard in the Andes. The bad conditions forced him to land his small plane. He started to walk, although he did not know in what direction he was going. He could not determine how far he was from other living beings, nor did he know if he would make it. He had nothing to eat or drink. When his shoes wore out, he threw them away. Frostbite set into his feet, and he started to grow tired. Hunger and thirst joined him, and he then began to wonder if it would not be better to lie down in the snow and never wake up again.

Then at that same moment, he thought of his wife. She waited for him back home. He knew that if he gave up and died there in the snow, his wife would never experience the happiness of his homecoming after such a long time. He knew she was probably thinking, "If he lives, he is certainly coming in my direction. He is flying, or walking, toward me because he loves me. If he lives, he walks. If he lives, he walks." Repeating these words over and over again, Saint-Exupery continued to walk until he fell unconscious in the snow and later woke up in a small hospital. Because of his wife who waited for him and whom he really loved, he survived.

Martin Gray is another example of a person who experienced much suffering. As a child, he lived in a Warsaw ghetto during World War II. From the age of fourteen, he was marked for extermination by the Germans. They forced him to wear an armband emblazoned with the Star of David, which identified him as a Jew.

Gray chose, however, to fight the Nazis rather than passively accept his fate. He risked his life to smuggle food to his mother and brothers, who hid behind a false cupboard in their Warsaw apartment. When the members of his family were betrayed and herded aboard a train for the infamous Treblinka concentration camp, Gray joined them in a rescue attempt. When he realized they had been murdered, he escaped and became active in the Polish resistance movement against the Nazis.

Gray constantly envisioned the day when he would overcome the Nazis and avenge his family's deaths. When at last he marched victoriously into Berlin as an officer of the Russian army, he was seized by the distress of the inhabitants. He saw in them his own sufferings. In his heart, compassion and the desire for revenge were waging a terrible struggle. How could he find a solution to this conflict between light and shadows, between love and bitterness, between pardon and hate?

While struggling with that conflict, he remembered his mother. Her love gave him strength in his suffering. She was a very gentle, quiet person who had no need to speak, for all her acts were full of love. When he entered the first enemy town, ready to avenge his family's murders, his mother's image held him back. When he and his fellow soldiers searched the town for the enemy, instead of enemy soldiers, they found only the very old and the very young. The memory of his mother held him back from any act of brutality and vengeance.

That day, Martin Gray took a decisive direction in his search for meaning. The memory of his family prevented violence from winning out over goodness and kindness. He realized that he had become incapable of revenge, for it would never restore his family to him. Death cannot be redeemed.

Gray's philosophy of life in the face of suffering is perhaps best expressed in his book *Le Livre de la Vie*. He writes that reason is not enough for us, but it is a start to a cultivated life. What really makes us grow (the water, as he puts it) is love, is others, is hope, and the belief that tomorrow is where beauty lies. He goes on to say that when suffering comes (and it does since death is imminent), there is also hope that the suffering leads to something much bigger, much higher, and more meaningful.

Stoics try to remain above suffering—to make an abstraction of it. Responsible human beings use their suffering to show love for others. To suffer is to dedicate oneself to others. Suffering must be linked to other people. Shared suffering makes us human. The same is true for happiness. Happiness is essentially being happy with and for others. Sharing happiness often gives more meaning to our own happiness, just as sharing in suffering gives more meaning to our own suffering.

Categories of suffering

There are different kinds of suffering, which may be experienced in various ways and degrees. The first is physical suffering. We can suffer physically from an illness, an injury, a tumor, from cold or heat, from fatigue or sleeplessness, having a leg amputated, experiencing a stroke, becoming partially paralyzed, losing eyesight, or suffering from multiple sclerosis. These are all difficult crosses to bear.

Another form of suffering is emotional suffering. It may be caused by the death of a loved one, rejection by a peer group, dissatisfaction with a job or lifestyle, or loneliness. Familial, marital, and mental problems, or worries about the past or the future may create deep sufferings that cannot be measured by objective standards or compared to the problems of others.

Spiritual suffering is yet another kind of suffering. It is the feeling we get when it seems that our lives are out of touch with God or that we no longer have faith in God. It is also the kind of suffering we experience when we feel our mortality or fear that we are great sinners.

Each of these kinds of suffering varies from person to person. They even vary within a single individual at different times and under different circumstances. But all these types of suffering are interrelated and influence one another. Spiritual or emotional suffering is usually an element of incidents dealing with physical suffering and experience. A person who loses his leg in an accident, for example, will suffer from it emotionally. He feels that he is not accepted by society. He may blame God for his loss and be angry that something so terrible happened to him for no reason. But everyone who suffers does not necessarily react in a negative way. Some people give us an example of acceptance, courage, and inspiration. Two examples of this stand out, both from my nursing-home experience.

George was a sick older man. He had diabetes, and both his legs had been amputated. His eyesight was severely impaired. He loved to talk about his experiences as General Patton's assistant. Although physically disabled, his clear mind could recount history in the making. This once very powerful person had to be fed by a nurse, and someone had to wipe his chin when he spilled his soup. All that he had left was there in his room—several pictures of his family, a watch pinned to his gown so he could see time, a chair from home strewn with several handmade pillows, and an afghan that the Veterans of Foreign Wars had given him. George had given all his war medals and honors to nephews when he moved into the nursing home. He said he enjoyed their visits, but because they lived out of town, they could not come very often.

Although he had been through much, George continued to set goals. He set a goal to get his diabetes under control and visit his nephew's home for Christmas. Not one word of complaint came from his lips. He was making plans to fight his illness in a systematic way and was full of hope and courage. He was an inspiration for the nursing-home residents and staff.

Another example is that of Loretta, an elderly bedridden woman who did not recognize her own children. She talked of her husband who had been dead for 25 years as if he were still living. Her life setting was a little room, with several family photos sitting on the bureau. Her children suffer a great deal to see her in that state. Loretta can communicate only by incoherent sentences, unintelligible words, and groans. But the attitude of her children—the manner in which they stood there, attentive but powerless—impressed the nursing staff. And certain ones have been able to consider their own suffering in another perspective. They have been better able to see their own ills in a more objective, relative way.

Many say that sickness and misfortune change people's personalities, that people become totally different when they endure suffering. Some people who were healthy and happy become angry and negative after a misfortune; others don't.

Suffering can change a personality, but it can sometimes reveal a realness, which differs from the masks we are used to wearing in all of our daily roles. We often just act in the roles of father, mother, husband, wife, teacher, waiter, doctor, lawyer, priest. It's easy to be the person we are supposed to be in a particular role at a particular time. How frightened we are, then, when one day we find ourselves face-to-face with our true "self."

Looking for the Meaning of Suffering

The meaning of all suffering doesn't exist. A general and universal meaning applicable to all kinds of suffering is impossible to formulate. Suffering is always very personal to our own experiences and, therefore, is always unique. Our suffering cannot be compared with the suffering of another human being because suffering is very subjective. One person will suffer more from a financial misfortune, for example, than another person whose suffering stems from the death of an only child.

If each person's suffering is unique, then the meaning found in that suffering will also be unique. This meaning relates to the psychology of the suffering person, to the circumstances, the time, and the kind of event that caused it. Some suffering may be more readily accepted as a part of being by an older person than if it had come at an earlier stage of life. People who have never suffered or who have never been in contact with suffering during childhood and adolescence will have more problems finding meaning when they experience any type of suffering at an older age. They will also be inclined to exaggerate their conditions.

Suffering is a lifelong learning process that begins the day we are born. This does not mean we will be able to carry our crosses without flinching or feeling pain, but this learning process will help us carry our crosses better. It is also important to expose children to experiences that will help them learn the value of suffering and the meaning that can come from suffering. Providing a totally closed-off existence for youngsters leaves them ill-prepared for real life because real life will not always be easy. There will be problems for everyone. Just as people must learn to love, they must learn to suffer. Coping with a little pain in a positive way helps us cope with greater suffering in other circumstances. Bad experiences are not utterly worthless as long as we learn from them.

Growth in suffering

There is an inherent contradiction in the phenomenon of suffering. In a certain way, we need suffering to learn and to grow into wiser adults. On the other hand, suffering and pain seem to be what we constantly try to avoid. As we grow, we will undoubtedly go through quite a bit of suffering—suffering in which we will have found meaning. To endure a crisis, to go through suffering and pain, often provides the strong foundation needed to become more human.

Finding meaning in suffering is a difficult and energy-draining process. It has different stages: shock, denial, anger, depression, and ups and downs. Then after a certain turning point, we are able to see light at the end of the tunnel. That turning point can come when we meet another person who is willing to go that extra mile with us on our way of the cross. It could also be a particular circumstance, for example, reading the Bible or a good book. Finding meaning in suffering almost always presents itself after a dark period, first in vague form, which then becomes more concrete every time we talk about it and try to formulate it; but it makes us human. This meaning, or purpose, will be a growing force that will become stronger and more deeply useful as time goes by.

"I had to believe," said a 45-year-old patient with multiple sclerosis, "that everything that happens in life happens for a purpose. Everything has a purpose and is meant for our good. I was a popular guy, loving cars and girls, and confident of making a lot of money. The discovery of my illness changed my life. God taught me a lesson. He made me more thoughtful, more sensitive to others. Before that, I never worried about others. God has purged me of my pride and arrogance. He made me better."

Finding meaning in suffering is a combination of effort and chance, or grace. If we want to find meaning in a painful circumstance, we must try at first to survive and to come out of the depressing situation. If we are not trying to do it, nobody can do it in our place. But if we are trying to do it, the grace of God will help us come out of the dark tunnel of suffering. These two factors, grace and human effort, will help us cope with and digest the suffering in a positive spirit. Grace is always amazing. This amazing grace is connected with God's role in our lives. The presence of the Holy Spirit in the life of each of us will push us to believe in that light at the end of the tunnel in an experience that causes suffering.

The meaning of suffering is not found in a response to questions like "Why?" and "Why me and not someone else?" No one can explain why a person has to suffer some particular misfortune. The meaning of suffering is found in the existential answers to the questions, "What can I do with it?" and "What can I make from the situation in which I find myself?"

For one young woman, the death of a child became the start of a meaningful life—a life full of generosity to the poorest of the poor in Africa. For another person, the suffering of a divorce helped her to be more herself and to believe more in herself. Some have learned to appreciate another more through the death of a common friend. Some have learned not to take another for granted when a relative or friend is dying. Many people waste life's most important gifts when, in self-pity, they insist on continuing to ask, "Why?"

What we see as a positive value in our sufferings is always very personal and unique. It can also be extremely inspirational for others. Experiencing any type of suffering always helps others to gain perspectives on their own experience. And sometimes that company in and of itself helps our own experience with suffering. The best attitude we can have in the face of suffering is a silent presence. This silence—just being with the other—will be the beginning of a healing process that will take its time. God's presence manifests itself mostly in silence through the grace of peace. Everything we suffer can have value and can produce good fruits, if not for ourselves, then for others.

Through their faith, Christians have a particular way of finding meaning in their sufferings. Christians believe in providence rather than fate. They believe that by doing God's will, they ultimately will be blessed. Their faith teaches them that they participate in Christ's sufferings for the salvation of the world. They believe that through their sufferings here on earth, they will have a better existence in the life hereafter.

Questioning why we suffer: a recent phenomenon

In the theological works of Augustine, Thomas Aquinas, Ignatius of Loyola, and Martin Luther, there is no mention of the problem of suffering as we see it today. Suffering seemed to be accepted in that time as a part of life. It was not a problem. Since the beginning of humankind the Bible has taught that we are surrounded by the voices of suffering, that we live in a "vale of tears." Christians were seen as "homeless people" in a secular world—always on an exodus, enduring the demands of hope and uttering the cries of suffering, because their final destination was heaven, and earthly life was only a passage.

In the course of this earthly pilgrimage, they endure pain and deprivations in the hope of arriving "in the house of the Father." More than others, Christians are convinced that suffering can be "liberating." After some great and painful struggle, one usually finds the deepest peace. Would that not be the same for Christians after our life here on earth? As we have already said, suffering can bring human beings together. Is it surprising, then, if Christians, searching for the meaning of their sufferings, find themselves together at the foot of the cross? In contemplating the cross of Jesus, we have a model of how to suffer, and this divine example can help us find meaning in suffering. It is there that we arrive at acceptance and at the conviction that one day suffering itself will be vanquished.

The Book of Job in the Old Testament gives us the best approach, enabling us to find meaning in life throughout our sufferings. Struck by a series of trials that deprived him of all his children and all his possessions, Job began by rebelling and scolding God. Little by little, however, he fell silent and began to see the beauty and the mystery of nature around him. He saw that God was good after all. Job understood then that knowing and accepting God was more important than trying to find answers that no human being can or could ever give.

The meaning of suffering and the meaning of life are aspects of the same human reality. One aspect adds to the dimension of the other. Without suffering, without crises and problems, many people will never discover the meaning of their own lives or even catch glimpses of some provisional meaning in their day-to-day living. And inversely, without things like meaning in life, values, and faith in God, faith in ourselves and in other human beings, no one will ever be able to detect meaning in suffering.

Living and waiting for an answer

Christians know that God never abandons a suffering human being. Nevertheless, being convinced of this divine presence does not suppress the suffering and the darkness, but it does help us to find the right attitude. The prophet Micah expressed it this way, "Though I sit in darkness, the LORD is my light." (7:8). And Job gives witness, "Oh, that I were as in the months past, as in the days when God watched over me: While he kept his lamp shining above my head, and by his light I walked through darkness" (29:2–3).

Suffering is and will always remain an enigma. This mysterious reality of pain contains, however, latent riches, as much for those who suffer as for those around them. So many ties bind us to others that no one ever suffers entirely alone. That is why our suffering can have liberating or debilitating consequences for them.

Our personal suffering can help others or push them into despair. That depends to a great extent on the attitude we adopt in the face of our suffering. Remember, above all, that our God is a God of love, anxious about our well-being and our happiness. God is always near, even if we let go of him. Our God is a God who helps us to develop our personality and to better manage the world in which we live. Jesus never promised us an easy life from which the cross would be absent; he did promise to stay near us during difficult times.

His example and his teaching help us to find meaning to our suffering and give us the courage necessary to carry our own cross. Let's not, therefore, repeat incessantly this "Why? Why?" Rather, let us be attentive to the questions that suffering itself asks us. Let our manner of accepting it be our response. Those who succeed in taking on suffering in a constructive manner do a great service, not only to themselves but also to others. Those who suffer bring a light that shines forth from their own darkness.

Suffering that hardens us and makes us bitter is like an accusation against God and humankind, as if they were responsible for our misfortunes. In his book *When Bad Things*

Happen to Good People, Harold Kushner, the well-known Jewish rabbi, invites us to ask the following questions when suffering enters our lives:

Can you forgive, or better yet, accept love in a world that has disappointed you (for it is not perfect)? Can you forgive or accept love and its imperfections because it is the only world we have?

Can you forgive or love the people around you, even if they have hurt you or left you abandoned (for they are not perfect)? Can you forgive or love them because they are not perfect and condemning them is like condemning yourself to loneliness?

Can you forgive and love God even when you are disappointed by a bout of bad luck or sickness? Can you learn to love and forgive God, like Job does?

If you do all of these things, can you recognize that the ability to love is the weapon God has given us to enable us to live fully, bravely, and meaningfully in this less-than-perfect world? [Text is paraphrased.]

Everything valuable and dear to us grows slowly. It always takes time and patience to realize something good and strong. Everything has its own *kairos,* its own "God time." That is what we read in Ecclesiastes: There is a time to live, there is a time to die, there is a time to rejoice, there is a time to suffer. But we like to forget that part about suffering. We will discover this *kairos* time if we are patient with ourselves, others, and God. It takes courage and patience to discover or rediscover it.

Reflections on Christian Spirituality in Older Age

During the period of old age, two opposing movements cross each other: a spiritual tendency toward the high and a physical tendency toward the low. Enough attention is paid to the tendency toward the low: the inexorable wear and tear on the body. However, the tendency toward the high is often neglected. By this expression, "The tendency toward the high," we mean to designate a growth of the spirit toward wisdom and interior freedom, toward plenitude, confidence, and pulling oneself together.

Though it's a matter of spirituality that

is appropriate to us in older age, let us begin by asking ourselves what the term *spirituality* means. After that, we will be able to draw that back to contemporary spirituality, saying something more specific on the spirituality of us in older age.

What does spirituality mean?

The word *spirituality* is related to the term *spiritual*, which lends itself to several meanings. According to most dictionaries, this term includes everything that has a connection with "the spirit," with the sacred, with religious values, or a supernatural reality. The term *spirituality*, then, concerns a "spiritual" disposition, a sensitivity and attachment to religious values.

These various connections, however, have a common point: they always have a certain rapport with a spiritual source of life and a desire for something that extends beyond our human nature. One always finds in it the desire for something larger or Someone more powerful who can lead us toward the full accomplishment of our existence, toward the discovery of a deeper meaning of this life. In the absence of this "something" or "Someone," there remains only a feeling of emptiness and of something unfinished.

No scientific method could define or describe with precision all of the richness of the concept of spirituality. Some speak of a supernatural order, attempting to make it tangible, while others, like Viktor Frankl, connect it more abstractly, as in a quest for meaning. This coincides with the search for meaning in our relations with nature, with others, and with God. In this light, spirituality would be a sort of realization of a distinct self in its desire for significant relations with the non-self, with others, with the Other.

This incessant search for that which has meaning is typically human. That is why theologian Henri Nouwen describes the spiritual life as "the heart of existence," the place where we are the most "human," where we are at the center of reality, where we discern for ourselves the significance of life and the finality of human existence.

We could just as well present spirituality as

an interior force that pushes us to look for and to find meaning and to express this meaning through religion, art, love, truth, joy, and suffering: in a word, through anything that transcends the material. Spirituality would then be this encompassing frame in which we reflect on the significance of all that is.

There exist, then, one could say, as many spiritualities as there are human beings on earth. Each must, in this vast frame and according to his or her temperament and capacity, seek his or her own way. Christian tradition, however, offers us examples that we can choose to follow in our spiritual growth. In this context, one will think, for example, of the spirituality of Augustine, of Benedict, of Francis of Assisi, of the Fathers of the desert, of the mystics, or—closer to us—of the spirituality of Charles de Foucauld, of Mother Teresa, of Abbe Pierre, of Thomas Merton, or of so many others. All these forms of spirituality are more or less bound up with a common determination for a deeper spiritual life, but each still touches upon different aspects of human sensibility. We can consequently ask ourselves,

What are the characteristics of contemporary spirituality, and more precisely, which spirituality would best suit persons who are growing old?

The multiple aspects of spirituality

Spiritual life is inseparable from the biological, social, or psychological aspects of existence. Taken as a whole, life is a subtle play of interactions, a coming and going of reciprocal influences of a corporeal, social, psychological, and spiritual nature. None of these factors exists in an isolated state. Thus our spiritual needs for growth are oriented and limited by our psychological, biological, and social needs. For example, it is difficult for us to meditate when we are hungry or thirsty, when our stomach is too full, or when we are tired. It is difficult to reflect, to taste an aesthetic pleasure, or to pray when the surrounding noise deafens us and when all sorts of external things distract us. Peaceful surroundings and a healthy body are favorable to meditation.

Biological and psychological needs can often coincide: we eat and drink at determined times, we celebrate on certain occasions, and most will agree that the same meal consumed in good company is so much more appetizing than when we dine alone.

Our Western turn of mind pushes us strongly to separate things, to analyze them, to dissect them—all of which ends sometimes in making a dead thing of reality. We continually set up barriers, we enclose ourselves, not only in our social life but also in personal and religious domains. We are often Sunday Christians, living in a manner hardly Christian during the week, treating certain people in a brutal and unjust manner, as though we were slaves of money and power.

We love to classify reality in opposing categories: black and white, body and soul, day and night, corporeal and spiritual, believer and nonbeliever. It is completely different in certain other cultures. The religion of an African accompanies him in his work, in the fields, in his family life, in his failures, and in his successes. If the harvest fails, he sees in it punishment from the gods. We would be inclined to speak of a primitive, irrational mentality, but who or what is primitive in this case? Are we sure of being right when we analyze quite rationally? It is important, therefore, to examine here the coherence of things, especially in considering (more closely) the relationship between spirituality and religion.

Spirituality and religion

Spirituality is not necessarily identified with religiosity. Spirituality is a larger category, it encompasses more. It has, however, connections with religiosity. Therefore, persons who live according to the spirit will be more accessible to the religious and, inversely, cannot live religiously without being open to the spiritual. Religion and spirituality are not always situated at the same level, and they both depend on other aspects of our lives to become more nurtured.

We have already said that spiritual life is bound up with all other aspects of existence, whether material, physical, psychic, or social.

Spirituality unifies them and gives them co-herence. Spirituality integrates these multiple aspects in the unique "self" that we are. And this "self" will never be able to be reduced to equations or to a system of index cards, for we are so much more than the sum of all these partial aspects.

The life of the spirit is, no doubt, the most profound spring of our activities, the source of our life forces. When it comes to matters of the spirit—in old age, especially—it should be "things" that we are ready to sacrifice, which can be very diverse from one person to the next. What is really important is not of the material realm, even of the realm of health. The most important "things" are, in fact, not even things; they are found in the domain of the interpersonal: to be close to those we love, to help others, to be recognized by others, to be able to express oneself through the spoken word or through writings or by means of different art forms.

Listening to music or playing it, writing or reading poetry, painting or admiring a picture, loving and being loved: these are all values of creativity and of experience that can be integrated according to the spirit and nourish the growth of our spirit in old age. In addition, they procure a profound joy and constitute points of support in times of suffering and difficulties. These spiritual activities are often prerequisite to being able to pray, to unite us with God.

After this brief reflection on the general term *spirituality*, we will now address the characteristics and the major lines of spirituality in contemporary society.

The tendencies of contemporary Christian spirituality

A contemporary Christian spirituality will be, first of all, closely tied to life, as attentive to the beauty and the goodness of this life as it is to its miseries and injustices. This tie invites us, on the one hand, to rejoice in all that is beautiful and good and, on the other hand, pushes us on to action and combat. Prayer is an important part of our contemporary spirituality (or, at least, should be). Many of our contemporary prayers reflect this double aspect. They are penetrated with a sort of mystique of the beautiful and with the sentiment of the protective presence of God, the All Good.

But these same prayers call us to struggle against the injustices of the world and therefore become a source of courage. Prayer is an effort for peace and justice, an effort to unite ourselves with God by means of the splendors of nature and the pain of human beings, beginning with calls for just that…justice and peace. Prayer improves our perception of all the aspects of human existence: joys or sufferings, wealth or poverty, liberty or injustice, hope or despair, success or failure.

Let's add that a Christian spirituality doesn't admit any limits; rather, it encompasses the entire world. Thanks to the facilities of travel, of the media, and of the improved means of communication, the entire world has become our village, our house. We know and we see what is happening near and far. Famine and sufferings in Africa, natural calamities in Asia, what is happening no matter where—

all is part of our daily lives. The events of the current world force themselves before our eyes and strike our hearts. We are invited to a growth in spirituality the size of this world.

Besides this wholistic sense, a contemporary Christian spirituality is characterized by its special attention to the poor and the weak. It is not only the fundamental theme of liberation theology, but quite simply that of any Christian spirituality. The call of the prophet Jeremiah is more timely than ever: "Because he dispensed justice to the weak and the poor, he prospered. Is this not to know me?—oracle of the LORD" (22:16). The parable of the Good Samaritan teaches us as well: Those who want to serve God must serve their brothers and sisters and go to their aid in their distress, without making a detour to avoid a hurt person.

At the same time, it is not easy for us to step out of our comfort zones, a position we are sure of, to plunge into the unknown and undertake a new spiritual life. But men and women in great numbers try this experience still today. How many new groups and communities do you not see appearing with their spirituality quite affirmed? Most often, these persons live their faith, meeting with the presence of God through their suffering brothers and sisters who have such great need of their help and presence.

Wasn't the most profound revelation of God realized in Jesus, the Man of Sorrows, and who, after his glorification, was called Christ the Savior? As disciples of Christ, we will be judged by those who suffer, by this sick person, by this slow-witted old man, by the starved of developing countries. This judgment will also be the judgment of the living God, of this God who stands before us in the clothing of the beggar and who knocks gently on the door of our hearts. He just knocks, without any violence, in the hope we will be willing to open the door to him.

Finally, it is important to point out the essentially social character of contemporary Christian spirituality. Human beings are never isolated individuals but social beings. Even those who try to live in a spiritual manner need others. They need a community that supports them, such as an ecclesiastic community, prayer and reflection groups, or teams of friends or housemates. It is in such groups, where we mutually support one another in faith, that we will be able to attain and celebrate the profound dimensions of existence. "Where two or three are gathered together in my name, there am I in the midst of them" (Matthew 18:20), the Lord Jesus promised us.

How to Develop Your Spirituality in Old Age

Do elderly persons need their own kind of spirituality? That is a question that often stays in the back of our minds and that many don't even think to ask. Of course, we are disposed to see that material comforts—physical well-being—of older persons are met, but we are less convinced of their need of a spiritual life. Would that be a consequence of our cursed Western activism? We are always inclined to ask ourselves, *Can I do something when there is nothing to do? Can I do anything else to increase comfort?*

Passivity: Slowing down

At the heart of spirituality for the elderly, one meets the word *passivity*, a word we often understand incorrectly. It should not be a matter of capitulating, of doing nothing, of letting ourselves go. The passivity we are talking about is, at its basis, confidence, putting ourselves back together. A spirituality for old age begins with a "yes," full of hope for the future. It is a confident acceptance of what will still come and the will to draw from it the best parts possible. Biological and psychosocial activities will regress certainly, but the spiritual can benefit from this. Old age can become the opportunity to discover certain aspects or new possibilities of existence and to live them fully. Our body weakens, but from the spiritual point of view, we can continue to progress until our last day.

The physical limitations as we age can even help us to better perceive true values—values such as beauty and goodness, love and union with God. We slow down physically, but this allows us to take time for what is really important; and only then will our rhythm of life seem truly meaningful, though we are tempted to think our lives are ineffectual. In these moments, go sit near persons who aspire to a little attention. Find the time for those dear to you. Isn't that an authentic sign of love, to take time to simply be there, without doing anything in particular?

One aspect of slowing down is not to run from one task to another, but to walk, to enjoy a bike ride, or to observe from the window the ballet of the seasons that is reflected in the leaves of the big chestnut tree and to observe too the beauty and goodness in humankind.

Passivity can take the form too of compassion. Our first reflex is to move away from the suffering of another, for it shocks us and we dread its touch one day. However, an attitude of sincere compassion is not centered on our own emotions or on our powerlessness but is concentrated on the suffering of the other.

Passivity is also receptivity: it is an attitude open before all that life and others can bring to us. Thus we should not close ourselves off to the attention, the warmth, and the comprehension we can give to others. We should, rather, remain available for all those privileged and significant moments of certain encounters or profound affection. This time of life offers so many possibilities and opportunities. Let's be able to welcome them.

Monks, perhaps, let us glimpse best what this passivity comprises. American author Paul W. Jones writes in an article on spirituality that during his stay at a Trappist monastery, he realized how opposite monks are of "modern" values. He compares their spirituality to those of elderly persons. They live against the fast-paced current, the noise-filled and agitated culture. They opt for silence and reflection. In a world of personal fulfillment, they renounce themselves. Success is not measured by wins and losses but by what is gained in both situations. They are not consumed by consumption. They do not value "information" but, rather, wisdom. In a complex culture, they invite us to look for only the necessary, and they remind us that a high level of life counts much less than the quality of life.

Some subversive lifestyles

Passivity coincides, then, with a way of living subversively, with an interest in values that are opposed to conventional models. This mode of life, which the monks test to the maximum, can render great service to aging persons as well. They will be able to find in it certain values of vital importance, which our modern society has more and more neglected.

The Bible teaches us that this passivity, well understood, is an attitude that suits aging persons. Did not Jesus say to Peter, "When you were younger, you used to dress yourself and go where you wanted; but when you grow old, you will stretch out your hands, and someone else will dress you and lead you where you do not want to go"? (John 21:18).

At first reading, these words are hardly encouraging, but it is a matter of the vocation we all have. We must "let ourselves go," have confidence in life and place ourselves in the loving hands of God. Then we will be able to go peacefully where we "do not want to go"— toward advanced age with its inevitable limitations, toward the breakdown and the death that, for a Christian, is never the last word; you will follow Christ beyond this life. Extend your hands and you will accept the "grace" that will be presented to you at every moment. Be open to the Spirit of God, which leads each of us where, as prisoners of egocentrism and selfishness, we fear to go.

We find this attitude of passivity again when Jesus speaks of the lilies of the field: "They do not work or spin. But I tell you that not even Solomon in all his splendor was clothed like one of them" (Matthew 6:28–29).

The subversive way of life also becomes a way to pray. Old age will then become the time when words will be replaced by a simple "being there" in the presence of God, in silence, in the feeling of our powerlessness. We will have renounced every anxiety about self-worth, about every ambition, about the pursuit of power and success. We will let ourselves be penetrated by this mysterious reality that supports us, by this God to whom, down the passing years, we no longer feel the need to give a name or a face, if it is not perhaps the name of Love and the face of the One who has been attentive to our sufferings. Will we say this is "mystical"? More simply, it is a question of living in the presence of God and of "letting ourselves go" to God in confidence.

This spirituality characteristic of aging persons not only leads to a happy flowering, it even permits the surpassing, the transcending of self. This passing beyond self will aid the aged in not letting themselves get entangled in the little nothings of each day, like what diet to follow, the way one has slept, little miseries or other annoyances.

A concrete spirituality

It is not enough to say that passivity, rightly understood, probably constitutes the nucleus of spirituality for old age. It is in concrete daily living that each of us must find valid applications for our case. The elderly are not called to glide over earthly contingencies, but to bear concretely all the inconveniences of life, to put up with others who have difficult dispositions, to give and to pardon, to aid and to serve. But we are called also to take advantage of the opportunities each new day brings. Don't look far away; each day and in whatever circumstance, the elderly will find opportunities to unfold their personalities.

This attention to the concrete will not impede our spirituality from opening itself to the dimensions of the entire world. Even aged persons habitually know quite well what is happening elsewhere in the world. To be able to cast an understanding and benevolent gaze on far-away events is also a characteristic of a strong spirituality.

Elderly persons who live "according to the spirit" will exercise a great influence on younger generations, showing them that life is more than incessant activity, more than ownership, power, success, and more than an irreproachable physique. And if the elderly invest in initiatives bearing on the protection of the environment, in projects favoring the quality of life in general, the younger generations can rejoice in it. The existence that awaits them in the next century will be that much more beautiful and rich, humanly and spiritually speaking.

Conclusion

The Bible presents a beautiful example of two elderly persons showing us the road to follow in the story of Simeon and Anna at the time Jesus is presented in the Temple. Simeon, a good and just man, was awaiting the coming of the Messiah. Anna was a widow who went to the Temple for hours each day to pray, and she would speak of the Messiah to anyone who would listen. The Holy Spirit had revealed to them that they would not suffer death before seeing the Savior. Simeon and Anna offer us a magnificent example of elderly persons who await the coming of Christ in the world, in their own heart, and in the heart of their neighbor. And we can now make ours the prayer of the aged Simeon: "Now, Master, you may let your servant go in peace, according to your word, for my eyes have seen your salvation" (Luke 2:29–30).

Elderly persons, animated by such spirituality, will find the gates of heaven wide open.

Ten Commandments
for a
Successful Old Age

1 Don't talk too much about your health and your little burdens. Only your physician is interested.

2 Take a good look at everything you do. If you let yourself be ruled by your little tics, you will find yourself doing bizarre things. You will put your eyeglasses in the refrigerator and you will use a bottle opener to lock the door!

3 Don't talk too much about your past accomplishments. People are more interested in themselves and in the future.

4 Take care of your external appearance. Wash and wear clean clothing. You will feel more sure of yourself and people will respect you more.

5 Detach yourself progressively from things and from people without ceasing to love them. That is the way of wisdom and the secret of dying well.

6 Appreciate solitude, and don't waste your time on futilities. Silence invites one to reflect and pray. You will be able also to develop your culture by reading or by exercising your talents: music, painting, embroidery, and so forth.

7 Note day-to-day in a notebook the principal events of your personal life and the reflections they suggest to you. This written account will help you in the long run to better know yourself and to better understand yourself and others.

8 Combat the effects of old age by not eating too much and by remaining active in spite of your natural sluggishness. You will thus preserve the vitality of your muscles and your brain.

9 Take an interest in the people you meet. Help them out as much as possible, but don't count too much on their gratitude.

10 Think with peace and serenity about your death that is approaching, but don't talk about it too often. Tell yourself that others await it in a future more or less near, and they even welcome it in certain cases.

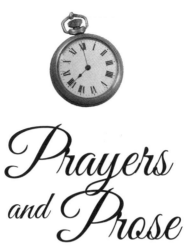

Prayers
and Prose

Prayer to Obtain
a Happy Old Age

Lord, my God,
Make of me to be poor in spirit,
Detached from all that I possess
And sufficiently diminished
To need you and others.

Make of me a compassionate being,
Sensitive to all suffering near or far away,
And saddened because so few
Recognize you, my God.

Make of me someone kind,
Who doesn't answer evil with evil,
And condemns no one
But who listens and tries to understand.

Give me always a hunger
For truth and justice,
To oppose untruth and deceit,
While still preferring love to my good reason.

Make my heart pure, simple, and true,
So that my "yes" be always "yes"
And my "no" really "no."

Make of me a peaceful and
  peace-making being,
Mindful of good understanding with others,
So that your peace may shine in me,
Even in incomprehension and contradiction.

And when the dark days come,
May I be able to continue in witness to you,
The God of my faith and of my hope.

For then, old and sick,
I will sense even better than today,
Your hand that sustains me and introduces
  me
Into that joy you have promised us.

Prayer of a Retired Person

God so good,
Here it is sixty-five years already that
    I am alive: a good half-million hours!
Upon rethinking of all that,
It seems to me that the time has passed
    with the speed of lightning!

Thank you, my God,
    for all that life has brought me.
Thank you because—
    oh! I'm not here for nothing—
You keep me in good health.
Each time I learn of the death
    of a friend or acquaintance,
I understand better
    how precious and fragile life is.
And I want to enhance fully
    every moment that is granted me.

That will be easier for me perhaps
Now that I am at rest.
Here I am, freed from the pressure
    of work and implacable schedules.

I can organize myself as I wish.
It is quite agreeable,
And I am grateful to you, my God.

Yes, my God,
     thank you for showing me so much love
Through the men and women
     who are good to me.
Thank you because I can believe in you,
For it is there that I find
     the meaning of my life.

Thank you for the hope and the confidence
That you give me each new morning.

Thank you, too, for these young people
     who are taking up my task
And are advancing on the roads
     I have mapped out.

Through all these gifts that I appreciate
And for which I give thanks to you,
You prepare me for this new life,
Close to you and in you.
Amen.

Prayer of an Aged
and Ill Person

Lord, my God,
Still another day!
Sometimes I no longer know very well
Where I am and who I am.
It is tiring to get up
And to let myself be cared for.
I hurt at the least movement
And I feel I am a burden for others.

Teach me to be good and kind
Toward those who live with me
And who care for me with tenderness.
Give me the gift to appreciate
    these gestures that soothe
And to recognize in them your loving presence.

Forgive me if I am sometimes blind
To the delicacy of others.
Pardon me if I forget the words you say to me,
Your words of consolation and encouragement.

Through all that I suffer,
Help me to become better,
And not ever to let bitterness and sourness
Settle in my heart.
Give me yet a little time to make up
For all that in the past I neglected
  or did badly.

Hold me fast, my good God,
Now that—as they say—
  I am "in my second childhood,"
And many treat me that way.
Keep me well hidden
  in the shelter of your Father's heart.

Prayer of an Aged Priest

It has not been easy to take leave
Of my parishioners and many friends,
To retire to this little room.

Here I am dependent on others,
I, who was lord and master in my rectory...
I was always afraid of being old,
And now I accept with difficulty
     all the restrictions
That are the consequence of old age.

Not long ago, I was an influential
     and highly thought-of man.
Now, do I still count?
If they listen to me,
     it is perhaps by politeness or by charity.

The perspective of my own death frightens me:
It is because of this that I sometimes dread
     to assist the dying.
I was convinced of the importance
     of the work and the action.

Now I must discover the mysterious riches
Of the last period of my life.

And then—I hardly dare say it, my God—
  this Christian faith,
  formerly solid as a rock,
  sometimes vacillates in me.
Where are you then, my God,
  when I cry out to you?
An entire life of devotion and of prayer
It wasn't all the same an illusion?

Show me then that you are my Shepherd,
I would like to feel your hand take mine
  when the darkness grows.

Help me to surmount this confusion, Lord.
Receive me just as I am.
Give me a little time yet
To prepare myself for the great meeting
  with you,
For it is for you that I have lived.

Prayer of an Aged Religious Sister

Here I am, seated near the window.
While the beads of my rosary
Slip between my fingers,
I often think again of the past.

I have worked much during my life,
All sorts of things humble and hidden
In the name of obedience.
My horizon was limited
    to the church and the convent.

Now that I have grown old,
The world seems changed and
    so strange for me...
Our convent is emptying,
My sister religious die one after the other,
And no one comes to replace them.

I ask myself sometimes:
Was it really worth the trouble
To give myself completely for that?

I feel useless and superfluous,
I no longer count in this world.
People no longer greet me very often,
They hardly give me a glance
    of commiseration.

But in my best moments, Lord,
I remember your word:
"If the grain of wheat fallen in the earth
    does not die,
It will bear no fruit..."
I, too, must die,
And my congregation, too, probably,
So that we bear fruit a hundredfold
And so that, here or elsewhere, are reborn
New forms of religious life.

I forget so often, Lord,
    That dying is a necessity and an art,
    Even for a religious congregation.
Lord, strengthen my faith in you.
And my confidence in the future
    of your Church.

Prayer of the Dying

God of life,
I know that I am going to die soon,
But in your goodness, you still hide from me
the day and the hour.
Around me, I see that my near ones
are distressed,
Perhaps more than I myself,
Thinking about the inevitable separation.
In the secret of my heart,
I have already said goodbye to them,
As well as to all that was dear to me.

Now my eyes look farther:
They already glimpse another world,
And my ears discern unknown melodies.
All my other senses have dozed off,
My entire body floats in the unreal.
But my spirit is preparing for a new beginning,
This new life that you, the living God,
Have promised us.

I cast a last glance on all the beautiful
*   and the good*
That life has reserved for me.
I realize now
That even the most painful moments
*   and the suffering,*
Were for me a source of blessings.

Thank you, my God, for my whole life.
Remain close to me
Now that the passage has become so near.

Stay close, too, to those who will be distressed.
May their pain become a thanksgiving,
May their ardor and their joy in living
*   be reborn.*
As for me, Lord, "Let your servant
Go in peace, according to your word."

Prayer of Pope John XXIII

My God,
I cannot deny the evidence:
I have entered into my old age.
My spirit protests
And would like almost to revolt,
For I feel young still and full of life.
But a glance in my mirror is enough
To dissipate all my illusions.

Here it is the moment of goodbyes.
The time that remains to me to live
Is perhaps not very long;
I am already at the threshold of eternity.
That is why I must hasten
Still to do much good.

At the prospect of his death
The prophet turned toward the wall and wept.
I do not weep.
No, I do not weep and I do not even want
To be able to begin everything over
In order to do better.

Everything I did badly,
Or less well,
I confide to your mercy.

Psalm 71

In you, LORD, I take refuge;
*   let me never be put to shame.*
In your justice rescue and deliver me;
*   listen to me and save me!*
Be my rock of refuge,
*   my stronghold to give me safety;*
*   for you are my rock and fortress.*
My God, rescue me from the hand
*   of the wicked,*
*   from the clutches of the evil and violent.*

You are my hope, Lord;
*   my trust, GOD, from my youth.*
On you I have depended since birth;
*   from my mother's womb*
*   you are my strength;*
*   my hope in you never wavers.*

I have become a portent to many,
*   but you are my strong refuge!*
My mouth shall be filled with your praise,
*   shall sing your glory every day.*

Do not cast me aside in my old age;
*   as my strength fails,*
*   do not forsake me.*
For my enemies speak against me;
*   they watch and plot against me.*

They say, "God has abandoned him.
*   Pursue, and seize him!*
*   No one will come to the rescue!"*

God, be not far from me;
*   my God, hasten to help me.*
Bring to a shameful end
*   those who attack me;*
Cover with contempt and scorn
*   those who seek my ruin.*

I will always hope in you
*   and add to all your praise.*
My mouth shall proclaim your just deeds,
*   day after day your acts of deliverance,*
*   though I cannot number them all.*

I will speak of the mighty works of the Lord;
*   O GOD, I will tell of your singular justice.*
God, you have taught me from my youth;
*   to this day I proclaim your wondrous deeds.*

Now that I am old and gray,
*   do not forsake me, God,*
That I may proclaim your might
*   to all generations yet to come,*
Your power and justice, God,
*   to the highest heaven.*

You have done great things;
*   O God, who is your equal?*
Whatever bitter afflictions you sent me,
*   you would turn and revive me.*
From the watery depths of the earth
*   once more raise me up.*

Restore my honor;
    turn and comfort me,
That I may praise you with the lyre
    for your faithfulness, my God,
And sing to you with the harp,
    O Holy One of Israel!

My lips will shout for joy as I sing your praise;
    my soul, too, which you have redeemed.
Yes, my tongue shall recount
    your justice day by day.

Saint Paul Envisions His Impending Death

The time of my departure is at hand. I have competed well; I have finished the race; I have kept the faith. From now on the crown of righteousness awaits me, which the Lord, the just judge, will award to me on that day, and not only to me, but to all who have longed for his appearance....

The Lord stood by me and gave me strength, so that through me the proclamation might be completed and all the Gentiles might hear it. And I was rescued from the lion's mouth. The Lord will rescue me from every evil threat and will bring me safe to his heavenly kingdom. To him be glory forever and ever. Amen.

(2 Timothy 4:6–8, 17–18)

Older age lasts too long
for those who are sad;
Goes too slow for those who wait;
Is too short for those who are happy;
But is eternal life for those
who love and are loved.

Bibliography

Leo Tolstoy. *My Confession, My Religion: The Gospel in Brief.* NewYork: W.W. Norton, 1983, p. 20.

Carl G. Jung, Collected Works, Vol. 6. *The Practice of Psychotherapy.* NewYork: Pantheon Bollinger Series, 1966, p. 83.

Martin Gray. *Le Livre de la Vie.* Paris: *Editions J'ai lu,* 1996, p. 214 (author's translation).

Harold S. Kushner. *When Bad Things Happen to Good People.* NewYork: Schocken Books, p.147–148.

About the Author

A keen expert on questions related to old age, **Leo Missinne** unites practical experience and scientific knowledge. Born in Belgium in 1927, a White Father, he was professor and dean of faculty of psychological and pedagogical sciences at the University of Lovanium (Kinshasa, Congo). After studies in the United States, he was named professor of gerontology at the University of Nebraska in 1971. As guest professor, he has taught in North America, in Asia, and in Europe. Numerous publications in the fields of gerontology and psychology round out his activities. Currently retired, Leo Missinne now works as the chaplain of a rest home for the elderly.